WASHOE COUNTY LIBRARY

3 1235 03214 4144

P9-CJS-272

19

DUE

Property
of
Gerlach
Library

READING POWER

EXTREME SPORTS ™

Bicycle Stunt Riding

CHECK IT OUT!

Kristin Eck

The Rosen Publishing Group's
PowerKids Press ™
New York

1

SAFETY GEAR, INCLUDING HELMETS, KNEE PADS, GLOVES, SHIN GUARDS, AND ELBOW PADS SHOULD BE WORN WHILE BICYCLE STUNT RIDING. DO NOT ATTEMPT TRICKS WITHOUT PROPER GEAR, INSTRUCTION, AND SUPERVISION.

For Mike

Published in 2001 by The Rosen Publishing Group, Inc.
29 East 21st Street, New York, NY 10010

Copyright © 2001 by The Rosen Publishing Group, Inc.

All rights reserved. No part of this book may be reproduced in any form without permission in writing from the publisher, except by a reviewer.

First Edition

Book Design: Michael de Guzman
Layout: Emily Muschinske, Shay Moskovitz

Photo Credits: p. 1 © Harry How/Allsport; pp. 5, 9 © Louis Dallagary; p. 7 © Jamie Squire/Allsport; pp. 11, 13, 15, 17 © Tony Donaldson; p. 19 © Shelly Castellano/www.tdphoto.com; p. 21 © Tom Hauck/Allsport.

Eck, Kristin.
    Bicycle stunt riding: check it out / Kristin Eck.—1st ed.
      p. cm.— (Reading power) (Extreme sports)
    Includes bibliographical references and index.
    Summary: Briefly describes the sport of bicycle stunt riding, including the necessary equipment and some of the tricks that stunt riders perform.
    ISBN 0-8239-5697-0
    1. Stunt cycling—Juvenile literature. [1. Stunt cycling.] I. Title. II. Series. III. Series: Extreme sports.

GV1060.154 .E43 2000
796.6—dc21   00-028586

Manufactured in the United States of America

Contents

It is fun to ride a bike.

Some people do tricks on bikes. Bicycle stunt riding is when people do tricks on bikes. Bicycle stunt riding is also called freestyle biking.

This is a stunt bicycle.

A stunt bicycle has
handles, pedals,
and pegs.

brake handle

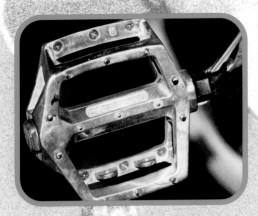

pedal

peg

This bicycle stunt rider is wearing a helmet, gloves, and knee pads to stay safe. Shin guards and elbow pads help, too.

13

Bicycle stunt riders do some tricks on the ground. This kind of bicycle stunt riding is called flatland.

Bicycle stunt riders do some tricks on ramps. They do tricks on rails or halfpipes, too. This kind of bicycle stunt riding is called vert.

This rider is turning the bike in the air. This trick is called a mega spin.

Lots of people like to watch bicycle stunt riding. Do you?

halfpipes (HAF-pyps) Ramps with high curved sides
and flat bottoms.

handles (HAN-dulz) Metal bars at the front of the bike that are
used to brake and steer.

helmet (HEL-mit) What a person wears to keep his or her
head safe.

pedals (PED-ulz) Levers that riders place their feet on to move a
bike or machine.

pegs (PEHGZ) Short metal tubes that stick out of a stunt
bicycle's wheels. A rider can balance on them to do tricks.

tricks (TRIHKS) Special, or difficult, moves or stunts.

Here is another book to read about bicycle stunt riding:

Bicycle Stunt Riding (Extreme Sports)
by Jason Glaser
Capstone Press (1999)

To learn more about bicycle stunt riding, check out this Web site:
http://www.espn.go.com/
extreme/xgames

Word Count: 136

Note to Librarians, Teachers, and Parents

If reading is a challenge, Reading Power is a solution! Reading Power is perfect for readers who want high-interest subject matter at an accessible reading level. These fact-filled, photo-illustrated books are designed for readers who want straightforward vocabulary, engaging topics, and a manageable reading experience. With clear picture/text correspondence, leveled Reading Power books put the reader in charge. Now readers have the power to get the information they want and the skills they need in a user-friendly format.